SOCCER BOOKS FOR KIDS 8-12

THE MOST AMAZING INSPIRATIONAL SOCCER STORIES FOR YOUNG DREAMERS

11
SAGAS OF
SOCCER STARS AND
THEIR BEGIN

CONTENTS

CONTENTS

INTRODUCTION

Once upon a time, in a world just like ours, there was a game. A game that was more than just a game. It was a dream, a passion, a way of life. It was called soccer. This game has seen many heroes rise from humble beginnings, heroes who have touched the stars and yet, have never forgotten their roots. This is the story of those heroes; the soccer stars whose lives and successes have inspired millions around the world.

Imagine a field, a green carpet stretched out under the open sky. It's not just any field; it's a battlefield where dreams are born and legends are made. The air is filled with anticipation, the crowd is roaring, and the heart is beating like a drum. This is the world of soccer, a world where magic happens.

In this world, there are no shortcuts or easy ways. It's a world that demands dedication, determination, and resilience. It's a world where the size of your dream matters more than the size of your shoe. It's a world where the only thing that counts is your love for the game.

Soccer is not only a game. It's an adventure, and it all starts with a single kick. No matter how big or tiny, every soccer player had the same beginning as you: a desire in their hearts and a ball at their feet. They encountered difficulties, stumbled, and fell, but they never gave up. They persisted in playing, dreaming and believing. They achieved greatness because of their commitment, resilience, and determination.

These soccer players are more than simply athletes; they also have voices. Voices that carry across the globe, inspire and empower others, and speak up for those who are unable to speak for themselves. They speak for a better tomorrow, for change, and for hope.

This book is a tribute to those voices, to those soccer stars who have achieved their goals. It's a journey through their lives, struggles, victories and legacy. It's a journey that will inspire you, motivate you, and show you that with perseverance, hard work, and commitment, you too can achieve whatever you dream of in life.

So, are you ready to step onto the field? Are you ready to chase your dreams? Are you ready to become a soccer star? Remember, the magic of soccer is not just in playing the game, it's in living the dream. No matter where you come from, no matter what challenges you face, if you have the passion, determination, tenacity and courage, you can make your dreams come true.

Welcome to the magical world of The most amazing inspirational soccer stories for young dreamers: 11 stories of soccer stars and their beginnings. Let's kick off this journey together. Let's dream, let's play, let's inspire. Because in the world of soccer, the sky is not the limit, it's just the beginning.

DID YOU KNOW?

Soccer Star Stories:

Lionel Messi: As a young boy, Messi was diagnosed with a growth hormone deficiency, but his determination led him to join FC Barcelona's youth academy after they agreed to pay for his treatment.

Cristiano Ronaldo: Ronaldo's first pair of soccer boots were hand-me-downs from his older teammates, which he had to stuff with newspapers to make them fit properly.

Sadio Mane: Mane used to travel 10 miles to practice every day because his village in Senegal didn't have a soccer field. He later built one for the community.

Kylian Mbappe: Mbappe's father was a professional soccer player and coach, which influenced his love for the sport. He donated his entire World Cup earnings to charity.

Pele: Pele's real name is Edson Arantes do Nascimento. He scored his 1,000th career goal on November 19, 1969, at the age of 29.

Luka Modric: Modric grew up in a war-torn Croatia and practiced soccer in abandoned buildings. He's also a talented accordion player.

Andres Iniesta: Iniesta comes from a small village called Fuentealbilla in Spain. His parents initially forbade him from joining Barcelona's youth academy because they thought he was too young.

Diego Maradona: Maradona was given his first soccer ball by his cousin when he was just 3 years old. He later became known for his famous "Hand of God" goal.

Curious Soccer Facts:

The fastest red card in soccer history was given just 2 seconds into a game.

The record for the most goals scored by a single player in a calendar year is held by Lionel Messi, who scored 91 goals in 2012.

The world's largest soccer tournament is the Gothia Cup in Sweden, featuring around 1,600 teams from over 80 countries.

The game of soccer was originally played with a pig's bladder, which is where the term "kicking the ball" comes from.

The oldest soccer ball in the world is believed to be from the 1540s and is made from a pig's bladder.

The most goals scored by a team in a single match is 149-0, with Stade Olympique de L'emyrne beating Adema in a 2002 game boycotted by Adema.

LIONEL MESSI

MAIN CAREER HIGHLIGHTS

World Cup: 1

Summer Olympics: 1

UEFA Champions: 4

UEFA Super Cup: 3

Spain Super Cup: 7

La Liga: 10

Copa del Rey: 7

Leagues Cup: 1

Copa America: 1

Lionel Messi: A Journey of Dreams, Determination, and Giving Back

Imagine a location where the scent of freshly cut grass permeates the air and the sound of a soccer ball bouncing reverberates like a happy tune. On June 24, 1987, a baby kid by the name of Lionel Messi was born in Rosario, Argentina. His story, it is a true journey that demonstrates how hard effort, dedication, and a caring heart can make dreams come true.

Lionel's journey began in a small house with a big heart. From the moment he could walk, he was dribbling a soccer ball. His love for soccer was like a secret code, one that only his heart understood. While other kids played with toys, Lionel played with his dreams. When Lionel was just six years old, he joined his local club, Newell's Old Boys. Despite being smaller than most of his peers, his extraordinary talent was undeniable. He would weave through the field like a tiny magician, his feet moving so fast that the ball seemed glued to them.

But achieving his goals wasn't easy. Growing Hormone Deficiency, a disorder that hampered Lionel's growth, was discovered when he was just 10 years old and threatened to put an early end to his soccer career. Some people thought that the fact that he was significantly shorter than his colleagues would prevent him from achieving his goals. Lionel, though, refused to allow his stature define him. With a passion that could match a lion's roar, he overcame each obstacle. Even though his family was unable to pay for the pricey procedure, Lionel persisted. He clung to his dream with unyielding determination.

Lionel used the soccer grounds in Rosario as his canvas and his moves as brushstrokes. He put a lot of effort into his practice that nearly appeared supernatural. Long after the sun had fallen, he would continue practicing his dribbles, passes, and shoots on the field Every setback, every doubt, only fueled his determination to prove himself on the grandest stage.

Lionel's brilliance was uncontrollable, like a fire. He was seen by scouts from FC Barcelona, a well-known soccer team in Spain, when he was just 13 years old. Because of his great impression, the scout set up a tryout for Lionel in Spain. The club saw his talent and volunteered to cover his medical expenses in exchange for his joining them. They were able to see what Lionel's heart had already known: that he possessed power that was just waiting to be released.

His journey to Spain was like stepping into a new world. Leaving behind family and friends, Lionel faced homesickness and a different language. But he didn't let these challenges deter him. He continued to play with the same passion that had guided him from the dusty streets of Rosario.

He worked hard, trained relentlessly, and never let his size or condition hold him back. His dedication paid off when he made his debut for Barcelona's first team at just 17. Lionel's journey with FC Barcelona was a whirlwind of victories, mesmerizing plays, won countless titles and record-breaking moments. From there, his career skyrocketed, he faced rivals who were taller and stronger, but none could match his determination leaving defenders bewildered and fans cheering with joy and with every goal he scored and every pass he made, he was rewriting the history books, his name forever etched in the annals of the sport and became one of the best soccer players the world has ever seen.

As Lionel's fame grew, he was given the opportunity to play for Argentina in the World Cup, putting him on the international scene. He carried the burden of the expectations of a whole nation with grace. He demonstrated that sports could bridge boundaries and bring people together in a common love of the "beautiful game" by playing with a passion that connected with supporters throughout the world.

Yet, amidst all the glory and his fame reached unimaginable heights, Lionel remained grounded, as humble as the kid who had once kicked a ball in the streets of Rosario. He never forgot his roots nor his town of Rosario, the place where he started to play. He carried his hometown in his heart, a constant reminder of the people who believed in him when he was just a boy with a ball and a dream. He always remembered the people who believed in him and the small town in Argentina where his journey began. He didn't let his accomplishments define him; instead, he let his character shine as a light of humility and gratitude. He knew that every success he achieved was a result of hard work, perseverance, and the support of those who had believed in him.

Lionel became more determined to have a positive influence off the field. With success, the Leo Messi Foundation helped youngsters in need all across the world. Lionel's foundation, which supported causes ranging from healthcare to education, was evidence of his conviction that success was not just about achieving one's own goals but also making a positive difference in the lives of others.

After that, Lionel Messi won his sixth Ballon d'Or, cementing his place in soccer history as a result of his unrivalled talent and commitment. He didn't only carry the trophy; he also clutched a tale as he stood there on that platform, surrounded by cheering spectators and his fellow teammates. A tale of a little child who, instead of letting his circumstances define him, made his goals come true and motivated millions of people.

He frequently travelled back to Rosario, returning as a hometown hero to the city that had fostered his aspirations. He made time for his loved ones and friends, as well as humanitarian activity that was very important to him. His life served as a testament to the value of maintaining ties to your roots and using your success to benefit those who paved the way for you.

Lionel Messi's story is a testament to the power of dreams, hard work, and perseverance. It shows us that no matter where we come from or what challenges we face, with dedication and commitment, we can achieve our goals. Lionel's journey was his ability to turn setbacks into comebacks. Injuries tested his resilience time and again, but each time he faced adversity, he emerged stronger and more determined than ever. His story taught the world that no obstacle is insurmountable, and no challenge is too great for a heart that refuses to give up.

So, children, remember Lionel's story, let it be a source of inspiration. Let it remind you that you, too, have the power to overcome challenges, achieve your dreams, and make a positive impact on the world. Just like Lionel, your journey is unique, and your potential is boundless. With determination, hard work, and a heart that cares, you can transform your dreams into reality and leave a lasting legacy of goodness and greatness. After all, every great journey begins with a single step.

DID YOU KNOW?

Soccer Star Stories:

Lionel Messi: Messi's first contract with FC Barcelona was when he was just 12 years old.

Cristiano Ronaldo: Ronaldo was expelled from school at the age of 14 after throwing a chair at his teacher who had insulted him.

Sadio Mane: Mane's father once chased away scouts who had come to recruit him, insisting that his education was more important.

Kylian Mbappe: Mbappe's mother was a former professional tennis player, and his father was a soccer coach. They emphasized a well-rounded sports education.

Pele: Pele's name was misspelled on his first jersey. He was supposed to be named after inventor Thomas Edison.

Luka Modric: Modric used to play soccer with friends using a ball made of rags in the war-torn streets of his hometown.

Andres Iniesta: Iniesta is a wine enthusiast and has his own line of wines produced from his vineyards in Spain.

Diego Maradona: Maradona once signed a contract with a club that included a clause to attend a weekly training session for a local youth team.

Curious Soccer Facts:

The fastest red card in professional soccer history was given in just 2 seconds to Lee Todd for foul language.

The highest number of goals scored by a single player in a single match is a staggering 16 goals.

The sport of soccer was responsible for the introduction of penalty kicks, which were initially known as "kick of death" in the 19th century.

In 1978, Iran had to play with a plain white kit in the World Cup because their usual kit's design was deemed disrespectful by the Iranian government.

The first soccer game ever broadcast on television was a friendly match between Arsenal and Arsenal Reserves in 1937.

The first player to be sent off with a red card in a World Cup match was Chilean player Carlos Caszely in 1974.

SERGIO RAMOS

MAIN CAREER HIGHLIGHTS

World Cup: 1

UEFA European: 2

UEFA Champions: 4

UEFA Super Cup: 3

Spain Super Cup: 2

La Liga: 5

Copa del Rey: 2

Ligue1 (France): 1

Trophee Champ: 1

Sergio Ramos: The Captain's Journey

In the sun-drenched city of Camas, Spain, a young boy named Sergio Ramos Garcia was born on March 30, 1986. From these picturesque streets, where the aroma of oranges filled the air, Sergio's journey into the world of soccer began – a journey that would see him rise to become one of the greatest defenders in the history of the sport.

Sergio grew up in a close-knit family, and from an early age, he had a deep love for soccer. His father, a construction worker, recognized his son's passion and built a small soccer field in their backyard. It was on this humble patch of grass that Sergio honed his skills, his dreams taking shape with every kick of the ball.

But life in Camas wasn't without its challenges. Sergio's family didn't have much, and buying the latest soccer boots or jerseys was a luxury they couldn't afford. Yet, Sergio's determination and love for the game were unwavering. He played soccer with anything that resembled a ball – oranges, socks, or even crumpled pieces of paper.

Sergio's potential was evident at the age of 14 and caught the eye of Sevilla FC, a well-known soccer team in Spain. The chance to pursue his aspirations required him to make a great deal of sacrifice, including leaving home at an early age. But Sergio accepted the challenge with his customary tenacity.

It was demanding to live in Sevilla FC's youth academy. Sergio was up against tough competition, and because of his youth and thin build, there were questions about his skills. He was not deterred, though. He committed himself to improving as a defender because he knew that with dedication and hard effort, any challenge could be conquered.

Sergio made his professional debut for Sevilla FC in 2004 at the age of 18. It was both the fulfillment of a dream and the start of a difficult path. He had to deal with the demands of playing professional soccer, where each game was a test of his abilities and moral integrity.

In 2005, Sergio's path brought him to Real Madrid, one of the most illustrious teams in the world. He would establish himself as a defensive team stalwart there. He was an unstoppable force on the field thanks to his exceptional heading skills, powerful tackles, and leadership abilities.

Sergio was extraordinarily successful during his career. With Real Madrid, he won four coveted UEFA Champions League championships in addition to multiple domestic league championships. He had a reputation for scoring important goals, especially with his head, and frequently served as both the club and national team captain of Spain.

However, Sergio's quest involved more than just self-actualization. Never forgetting his roots was the message. He stayed in touch with Camas, where his family and friends were still there to help him. He financed initiatives to upgrade the soccer facilities in his area and utilized his achievements to motivate the following generation of soccer players. He has been a UNICEF ambassador since 2014 and has been collaborating with ONGs since 2007 in which he has participated in different humanitarian project to protect kids in need.

Sergio's tale serves as proof that aspirations can come true with dedication, persistence, and hard work. It serves as a reminder that no obstacle, no matter how formidable, can stop someone who has faith in themselves and is prepared to work hard to realize their dreams.

As you read about Sergio Ramos' journey, let it inspire you to chase your own dreams with unwavering determination. Let it remind you that no matter where you come from, with passion and hard work, you can reach the highest peaks of success. Sergio's journey is a shining example of how children, like you, can achieve greatness through dedication and a never-give-up attitude.

DID YOU KNOW?

Soccer Star Stories:

Lionel Messi: He holds a Guinness World Record for the most goals in a calendar year.

Cristiano Ronaldo: Ronaldo's incredible leaping ability allows him to jump higher than the average NBA player.

Sadio Mane: He is a devoted Muslim and often celebrates goals by pointing to the sky in gratitude.

Kylian Mbappe: He is a polyglot, fluently speaking French and English and conversational in Spanish.

Pele: Pele played his last professional match for the New York Cosmos in 1977, attracting a massive crowd.

Luka Modric: He is an avid fan of kayaking and often enjoys the sport on the Adriatic Sea.

Sergio Ramos: He has a partnership with a winery in Spain, producing his brand of wine.

Diego Maradona: Maradona had an asteroid named after him, called "128858 Maradona.

David Beckham: Beckham has a passion for collecting old typewriters and owns a vintage collection.

Mesut Ozil: He contributed to a crowdfunding campaign to provide surgery for a young Arsenal fan.

Neymar: He holds the record for the fastest goal in Olympic soccer history, scoring just 14 seconds into a match.

Curious Soccer Facts:

In 1964, a referee sent himself off during a match after getting frustrated with his own decisions.

Soccer balls used to be brown, but they changed to white in 1951 for better visibility on black-and-white television.

In 2002, the African country Senegal made a historic run to the World Cup quarter-finals, led by players like El Hadji Diouf and Papa Bouba Diop.

The largest soccer ball ever made was 48.89 meters in circumference, created to celebrate the 2014 World Cup.

In 1996, a New Zealand goalkeeper named Jason Batty scored a goal from a free-kick, covering a distance of 95 meters.

The fastest goal in Premier League history was scored by Shane Long of Southampton in just 7.69 seconds against Watford in 2019.

The most goals scored by a single player in an official match is 16, achieved by Stephan Stanis of Racing Club de Lens in 1942.

EDSON ARANTES (PELE)

MAIN CAREER HIGHLIGHTS

World Cup: 3	Camp Paulista: 10
Copa Libertadores: 2	Tomeio Rio: 3
Intercont Cup: 2	NA Soccer League: 1
Inter Super Cup: 1	NA Atlantic L : 1
Camp Brasilero A: 6	

Pele: The Journey of a Soccer Legend

On October 23, 1940, a baby was born in Três Coraçes, Brazil's bustling and energetic streets. Edson Arantes was his real name, but the world quickly came to know him as Pele, a name that would come to stand for soccer brilliance, inspire a generation, and have a lasting impact on the game. His mother was a housekeeper, while his father, a former soccer player, worked as a janitor. Despite their difficulties, the family was warm, loving, and united by a love of soccer.

From a young age, Pele showed an extraordinary talent for the sport. He would spend hours playing soccer with his friends, using a sock stuffed with newspaper as a makeshift ball. His father, recognizing Pele's potential, began coaching him, teaching him the techniques he had learned during his own soccer career. As a young boy, Pele's life was colored by the rhythm of soccer. The ball was his constant companion, and the streets of his hometown were his playground. From sunrise to sunset, he would kick the ball with friends, mastering dribbles, practicing shots, and dreaming of one day playing on the grandest stages of the sport he loved.

Pele's life, though, wasn't all silky passes and flawless goals. He had difficulties as a child growing up in a poor home that would have prevented him from achieving his goals. The fields he played on were frequently nothing more than clumps of unlevel grass, and soccer shoes were more than a luxury. However, Pele's attitude remained unwavering, and while he played barefoot, his feet danced with tenacity. He used the love of the game to drive his endurance.

Early in his adolescence, a local scout identified Pele's ability and offered him a seat in the Santos FC development academy. Although it was a dream come true, doing so required him to leave his family and the comfortable surroundings of his hometown. At the academy, Pele had several difficulties. He battled with thoughts of homesickness and was younger and smaller than most of his contemporaries. He didn't let these challenges stop him, though. He put forth a lot of effort, trained more, and gave every game his all.

His dedication paid off when, at the age of 15, Pele was promoted to the Santos FC senior team. He was the youngest player in the team's history, but he quickly proved that he was also one of the most talented. His extraordinary skills, coupled with his humble and respectful demeanor, earned him the admiration and respect of his teammates and fans alike. Pele joined the Football Club, a step that would change his life forever. The world of professional soccer opened its doors to him, but the journey to the top was anything but easy. He faced skeptics who doubted his young age and untested abilities. Yet, Pele's resolve was unwavering, and he knew that his journey was just beginning.

During the 1958 World Cup in Sweden, Pele's brilliance was first seen by the world. He dominated the world arena at the young age of 17, astound viewers with his talent, quickness, and penchant for hitting the back of the net. He led Brazil to victory and became the youngest player to win the World Cup by scoring six goals during the competition. He scored twice in the semifinal and a hat-trick in the championship game. This was only the start of a career that would include many achievements and records.

Pele had difficulties despite his achievements. Critics questioned if he could maintain his brilliance in the face of injuries that threatened to sideline him. However, Pele's journey was characterized by tenacity. He put forth a lot of effort to become better, get back in shape, and keep demonstrating that he wasn't simply a one-tournament wonder.

As Pele's star continued to rise, his impact went beyond the field. He became a symbol of hope for his countrymen, a source of pride for Brazil during both triumphs and struggles. His skill and sportsmanship showed the world the beauty of soccer, and his humility endeared him to fans everywhere. He understood the significance of his roots, and his journey was a testament to the idea that dreams could be realized with hard work, no matter where one came from.

Beyond the soccer field, Pele's legacy included giving back. He established the Pele Foundation, an organization dedicated to supporting children's health and education. He understood that his influence could be a force for good, and he was determined to create a positive impact in the lives of those less fortunate. He used his platform to inspire and uplift, demonstrating that success was not a solitary pursuit.

As his illustrious career came to an end, Pele's legacy was firmly cemented. He was not just a soccer legend; he was an embodiment of the power of dreams and the importance of using one's success for the betterment of society. His journey showcased the essence of determination, the value of humility, and the significance of cherishing one's roots.

So, young readers, as you follow Pele's journey, let it remind you that dreams are within reach, no matter your circumstances. Let his story inspire you to chase your aspirations with unwavering commitment, to face challenges with resilience, and to embrace the responsibility of giving back to your community. Like Pele, you have the potential to make your dreams come true through hard work, dedication, and the belief that with perseverance, even the loftiest goals are achievable.

DID YOU KNOW?

Soccer Star Stories:

Lionel Messi: Messi's first coach at Barcelona, Xabier Mancisidor, used to bring him a special packed lunch every day since Messi's small size made him susceptible to fatigue.

Cristiano Ronaldo: Ronaldo used to practice his free kicks by aiming at a neighbor's washing line and trying to hit it with the ball.

Sadio Mane: Mane's pre-game ritual includes cleaning his own soccer boots as a way to remember his humble beginnings.

Kylian Mbappe: Mbappe's father, a former soccer player, had an unusual training regimen for him which involved running through a maze of ladders and cones.

Pele: made his professional debut for Santos FC in Brazil when he was only 15 years old. He scored a goal in his first match, setting the stage for his legendary career.

Luka Modric: Modric initially struggled with homesickness when he first joined Dinamo Zagreb's youth academy and missed his family and dog.

Andres Iniesta: Iniesta's parents initially discouraged him from pursuing soccer professionally and preferred he focused on his studies.

Diego Maradona: Maradona's pet during his Napoli years was a white stallion named "Bura."

Curious Soccer Facts:

The longest penalty shootout in soccer history took place in 2005 when Carabobo FC defeated Atlético Venezuela 20-19 in the Venezuelan Cup.

The first soccer match ever recorded took place between two teams of English schools in 1863.

The quickest sending-off in World Cup history was just 56 seconds into the match, when Uruguay's José Batista was red-carded against Scotland in 1986.

The shortest soccer player to play in a World Cup was Manuel "Manolo" Cáceres of Paraguay, who stood at only 5 feet 4 inches (1.62 meters).

The ball used in the 2010 World Cup in South Africa, called the "Jabulani," was criticized by players for being too unpredictable and hard to control.

In 2002, Australian soccer player George Weah was elected as the President of Liberia, becoming the first and only World Player of the Year to become a head of state.

MESUT OZIL

MAIN CAREER HIGHLIGHTS

World Cup: 1

UEFA Europea U21: 1

FA Cup: 4

Spain Super Cup: 1

La Liga: 1

Copa del Rey: 1

Leagues Cup: 1

Mesut Ozil: The Assist King's Journey

On October 15, 1988, a small kid named Mesut Ozil was born in the center of Gelsenkirchen, Germany. He would develop into one of soccer's most talented playmakers, famed for his amazing vision, deft passing, and inspirational journey that would encourage prospective players all over the world.

In a working-class neighborhood where the streets served as soccer grounds and hopes extended higher than the apartment towers, Mesut's story first began. His father, a former player and coach, fostered his talent, and his enthusiasm for the game was clear as soon as he could walk. Mesut and his father would talk for hours when the ball was at Mesut's feet, and dreams would take flight.

But Mesut faced challenges on his path to the soccer elite. He was a second-generation immigrant of Turkish ancestry who struggled with issues of identification and belonging. The soccer field became his sanctuary, a place where he could express himself and where his talent overcame any bias or skepticism.

Because of his very small size, Mesut had early concerns about his ability to play in the physically demanding sport of soccer. He made up for his lack of bulk, though, with skill, intellect, and a natural grasp of the game. His ability to see passes that others couldn't, to create opportunities with a flick of his foot, set him apart from his peers.

Mesut made his professional debut for Bundesliga with Schalke 04 at the age of 17. It was a dream come true, but it also heralded the start of fresh difficulties. From the streets of Gelsenkirchen, the pace and intensity of professional soccer were a considerable improvement. Mesut had to adjust right away, and he did.

When Mesut joined the German national team in 2010, his path took an international turn. He became a crucial member of a youthful, energetic team. His actions throughout that year's FIFA World Cup were nothing short of amazing. Germany advanced to the semifinals thanks to his dazzling assists and outstanding on-field poise, and he was given the Golden Boot as the competition's top young player.

Mesut's path did, however, include some highs and lows. A high point came with his move to Real Madrid, where he competed against some of the best players in the game. However, it was also a place with a lot of scrutiny and strain, where the burden of expectations might be debilitating. Mesut's mental fortitude was put to the test by challenges and criticism.

But he persisted. He revitalized his career after joining Arsenal in the English Premier League. He earned the moniker "Assist King," frequently topping the league in assists. Fans and fellow players were in awe of his remarkable playmaking ability. Mesut demonstrated to the world that no challenge was insurmountable and that failures served as steppingstones to achievement.

Mesut never lost sight of his origins during his travels. He continued to have ties to Gelsenkirchen, where his loved ones gave him assistance. He also celebrated his Turkish background and made use of his influence to support causes related to children's health and education. His voyage served as a reminder that success was more than simply personal accomplishment; it also involved having a good effect on other people's lives. Mesut has been recognized as one of the biggest soccer stars who has donated a lot of money for children education, charities and health in his root's country of Turkish.

As you learn more about Mesut Ozil's life, let it to motivate you to pursue your goals with zeal and commitment. Let it serve as a reminder to you that no ambition is too large to pursue and that skill and hard work make a winning combination. Like Mesut, you possess the ability to overcome obstacles, to accept your individuality, and to utilize your accomplishment to change the world for the better. Mesut's path is evidence that even the most ambitious goals can be achieved with dedication, hard effort, and a never-give-up mindset.

DID YOU KNOW?

Soccer Star Stories:

Lionel Messi: Messi has a collection of over 3,000 soccer jerseys from different clubs and countries.

Cristiano Ronaldo: He often surprises his fans by donating millions to various charitable causes.

Sadio Mane: Mane once missed a team meeting at Liverpool because he was busy helping to fix the roof of a local school.

Kylian Mbappe: He is the youngest player to score in a World Cup final since Pelé.

Pele: He composed and sang his own songs, including "Cidade Grande" and "Esperanca."

Luka Modric: Modric was named "Croatian Footballer of the Year" a record seven times.

Sergio Ramos: Ramos holds the record for the most goals scored by a defender in La Liga.

Diego Maradona: Maradona was an honorary citizen of Naples, Italy, due to his legendary stint with Napoli.

David Beckham: He participated in a charity motorcycle ride across Brazil to raise funds for children in need.

Mesut Ozil: Ozil is a skilled chess player and has played against world champion Magnus Carlsen.

Neymar: Neymar has a private tattoo artist who travels with him to ensure he gets fresh ink wherever he goes.

Curious Soccer Facts:

Soccer is played on every continent and is the most popular sport in the world.

The fastest goal in soccer history was scored just 2.5 seconds into the game.

The first international soccer match took place between England and Scotland in 1872.

Pele is the youngest player to win a World Cup, achieving this feat at the age of 17 in 1958.

The most red cards given in a single soccer match is 36, during a game between Sportivo Ameliano and General Caballero in Paraguay.

Uruguay won the first World Cup in 1930, and the captain of the team, José Nasazzi, was an accomplished violinist.

CRISTIANO RONALDO

MAIN CAREER HIGHLIGHTS

Premier League: 3

Football League: 2

UEFA Champions: 4

UEFA Super Cup: 2

Spain Super Cup: 2

La Liga: 2

Copa del Rey: 2

Cristiano Ronaldo: The Unstoppable Journey of a Soccer Legend

In the enchanting landscapes of Funchal, a coastal city on the island of Madeira, Portugal, the sun-kissed waves whispered secrets to the winds, and dreams danced on the sea breeze. It was here, on February 5, 1985, that the world welcomed Cristiano Ronaldo – a name that would resound through stadiums and inspire millions across the globe. His parents, Maria Dolores and Jose Dinis, worked hard to provide for Cristiano and his siblings. But his journey, far from a fairy tale, was a symphony of passion, grit, and an unyielding determination to rise above every challenge.

Cristiano's feet appeared to be drawn to a soccer ball magnetically from the minute he could walk. He would manage fictitious opponents with a skill that seemed beyond his years on the cobblestone streets of Funchal, which served as his playground. His initial steps on the road to stardom were witnessed by the surrounding fields, which were uneven but full of hopes. Even back then, his heart pounded in time with the rhythm of his goals and his feet moved in perfect unison with the ball. With every kick, dribble, and deafening applause that followed his plays, his friends were in awe of his talent, and his family saw the glimmer of something remarkable in his eyes.

However, Cristiano's path wasn't always clear. His family was struggling to make ends meet due to their financial situation. His parents, however, always supported his aspirations. His mother would frequently remind him: "Cristiano, everything is possible if you put in the effort and have confidence in yourself. These remarks spoke volumes to Cristiano. He practiced nonstop, frequently playing soccer until dusk and the turn on of the lighting. The fields he played on were far from ideal; there were clumps of crooked grass where, amid the flaws, fantasies grew. He played barefoot since shoes were an extravagance, and his determination overshadowing the discomfort. Although the path wasn't easy, Cristiano's passion was unwavering; he was determined to succeed despite the difficulties.

The path to achievement, however, was not without obstacles. The difficulties were as genuine as the hopes that kept him going. His tenacity was only strengthened by his limited resources. His feet moved in a symphony of effort and perseverance as he practiced nonstop, his sights firmly fixed on a future brimming with opportunities. Instead of discouraging him, the difficulties just contributed to the story of his journey, which was becoming more and more difficult to ignore.

His commitment wasn't overlooked. He was discovered when he was barely 12 years old by Sporting Lisbon, one of the top soccer clubs in Portugal. Cristiano travelled to Lisbon to follow his passion, leaving his family behind. Young Cristiano had a difficult time adjusting to life in Lisbon. He was really homesick and missed his family. In addition, he frequently felt uncomfortable and was made fun of for his

Madeiran accent. Under the direction of coaches who saw his potential, the promise he had displayed on the streets of Funchal developed into full-fledged brilliance. Cristiano's spirit was unshakeable despite the difficult trials, rigorous training, and severe competition. He never allowed these challenges get in the way of his goals. He had an unwavering commitment to his job and a strong self-belief, both of which were evident in the perspiration he produced on the practice field. He stayed committed to his objective, working harder than ever to hone his talents. His determination to put in the effort and fully commit to the game he loved marked his path.

Cristiano's dedication paid off when, at the age of 16, he was chosen to play for Sporting Lisbon's first team. Sir Alex Ferguson, the head coach of Manchester United, one of the largest soccer clubs in the world, was impressed with his performance. Sir Alex recruited Cristiano to play for Manchester United after being impressed by his skill and potential.

The path of destiny led him to the bustling stadiums of England, where he faced a new set of challenges. The English Premier League was a different beast, and the initial doubts lingered in the minds of skeptics about his adaptation to English football, new country and dealing with the immense pressure of playing for a top club but for Cristiano all those were like sparks that fueled his fire, he never forgot his mother's words. Cristiano, never one to shy away from adversity, embraced the opportunity to prove himself once again. He knew the world was watching, but he was ready to showcase his brilliance. And showcase, he did. With every sprint down the field, every tackle, every perfectly timed header and every goal, he erased the question marks and replaced them with exclamation points of triumph, etching his name into soccer history. He worked hard, believed in himself, and slowly but surely, he became one of the best soccer players in the world.

His path was a symphony of achievements and records broken. He outpaced defenders, electrified stadiums with his quickness, and displayed talents that astounded his opponents. Each goal was more than simply a point on the scoreboard; it was a symbol of his commitment and unyielding drive to break through barriers and redefine what was thought to be possible. Cristiano's humility, though, was a continuous reminder that his accomplishment was only a small part of the tale despite the acclaim.

As his star rose to dazzling heights and despite his success, Cristiano's connection to his roots remained unbreakable. He returned to Madeira, not as a superstar, but as a son of the soil who had conquered the world. The island that had witnessed his first steps now celebrated his every stride. He knew he was a role model, a symbol of hope for the children who shared his dream, and he embraced that role with a sense of responsibility that was both humbling and empowering.

Cristiano's journey wasn't just about his success; it was about the legacy he was crafting. With each triumph, he reached back to help others climb the ladder of opportunity. He understood that greatness wasn't measured solely by goals scored, but by the impact one had on the lives of those less fortunate. He often spoke about his humble beginnings and the struggles he faced. He also gave back to his community, donating to charities in Madeira, the Cristiano Ronaldo Foundation was his platform of change, his way of creating a ripple effect of goodness in the world.

His journey took him across borders, from England to Spain and beyond, but every chapter was a testament to his dedication. And when he returned to Manchester United, the cheers from fans were not just for a player; they were for an inspiration, a living example of what could be achieved through perseverance.

So, as you delve into Cristiano Ronaldo's story, let it be a reminder that dreams, no matter how audacious, are attainable with hard work, determination, and an unwavering spirit. His journey should inspire you to chase your aspirations with vigor, to conquer obstacles with resilience, and to embrace the responsibility of helping others along the way. Like Cristiano, you have the ability to script your own journey of achievement and impact, crafting a narrative that not only reflects your personal triumphs but also radiates kindness, just as Cristiano Ronaldo's journey continues to illuminate the world.

DID YOU KNOW?

Soccer Star Stories:

Lionel Messi: Messi was offered a chance to join River Plate's youth academy as a child, but his family couldn't afford the relocation costs.

Cristiano Ronaldo: Ronaldo's father named him "Cristiano" after U.S. President Ronald Reagan, whom he admired greatly.

Sadio Mane: As a child, Mane used to play soccer with a ball made of tied-up plastic bags in the streets of Senegal.

Kylian Mbappe: Mbappe's father, a former professional soccer player, banned any soccer talk at home to allow Kylian to develop a balanced childhood.

Pele: Pele's real name, Edson, was inspired by Thomas Edison, the famous inventor.

Luka Modric: Modric's grandfather was a military commander during the Croatian War of Independence, and his father was a mechanic.

Andres Iniesta: Iniesta's family had a hard time affording the transportation costs for his early soccer practices, and the coach helped out by picking him up.

Diego Maradona: Maradona's famous "Hand of God" goal was scored using his left hand, despite being right-footed.

Curious Soccer Facts:

The fastest goal in soccer history was scored just 2.5 seconds into a match when a player kicked off and found the net directly.

The record for the longest unbeaten streak in soccer history is held by ASEC Mimosas, a club from Côte d'Ivoire, with 108 games without a loss.

The soccer field wasn't always rectangular; early forms of the game were played on fields of varying shapes and sizes.

In 1964, Australian soccer team Adelaide Juventus played a match with just 7 players due to injuries and still won 2-0.

In the 1966 World Cup, North Korea reached the quarter-finals, beating Italy along the way.

SADIO MANE

MAIN CAREER HIGHLIGHTS

Africa Cup: 1

Premier League: 1

UEFA Champions: 2

UEFA Super Cup: 1

EFL Cup: 1

FA Cup: 1

Arab Cup: 1

From Dust to Glory: The Inspiring Journey of Sadio Mané

A little kid named Sadio Mané used to run barefoot over the dusty streets of the small Senegalese town of Bambali after a rusted-out football. Sadio, who was born on April 10, 1992, into a poor household, represented the hopes and aspirations of the whole hamlet. His mother made a living by selling products at the neighborhood market, while his father worked as a farmer.

Sadio had an insatiable enthusiasm for soccer from a young age. The village children would assemble in open fields, creating improvised goals out of logs and stones, and play competitive games that lasted until the sun set. Although he lacked the right equipment and formal instruction, his natural skill was obvious. Sadio rapidly stood out due to his natural talent and tenacity. Even though he was among the younger players, his persistently chase of the ball left older rivals in awe.

However, life was far from easy for young Sadio. The nearest proper football field was miles away. Sadio's first football was patched up more times than anyone could count, a testament to his unyielding determination. His family was skeptical about his dreams of becoming a professional soccer player. They urged him to concentrate on his schooling because they thought it would lead to a more stable future. He would frequently train alone, developing his abilities despite the odds by kicking the ball against the walls of their poor home and avoiding traffic in the winding streets of Bambali.

Sadio's dreams frequently posed a threat of failure due to financial issues. There were times when he had to decide between playing with his favorite ball and earning money for the family. Before heading to the football field to spend hours polishing his art, he would get up early in the morning to assist his father in the fields.

Sadio's abilities were soon recognized. A local coach noticed his commitment and natural talent and saw his potential. With the help of his coach and the community, Sadio left his village at the age of 15. When he enrolled in the Generation Foot academy in Dakar, the capital of Senegal, Sadio's adventure advanced significantly. The institution has a reputation for developing young talent and providing them with a stage on which to display their abilities. This was a crucial time that needed sacrifice from Sadio as well as his family, who pooled their funds to support him in following his ambition. But things were difficult at the academy. Sadio struggled with homesickness while adjusting to a new place, new people, and a new way of life.

Life at the academy was far from luxurious. Sadio shared cramped dorm rooms with other aspiring footballers and adhered to a rigorous training schedule. He often had to adjust to the fast-paced life in the capital city, far removed from the quiet simplicity of Bambali. But despite of the challenges, his determination and dedication remained unshakeable, and he poured his heart into every training session and match.

Sadio's efforts were not in vain; scouts from the Ligue 2 team Metz in France were drawn to him by his displays and extraordinary potential at Generation Foot. He moved to European football in 2012 at the age of 19, leaving his family and the community that had helped develop him. The journey was not without its bumps. Language hurdles, cultural differences, and the tremendous pressure of performing at such a high level were challenges that Sadio had to overcome. But his tenacity, work ethic, and humility won him the respect of both his colleagues and coaches, and eventually the effort paid off. With each game, his performances became better, and bigger teams quickly became interested in him.

Sadio's adventure only got better after that. He relocated to Red Bull Salzburg, where his lightning-quick pace, flawless dribbling, and eye for goal captured the attention of fans around Europe. He was transferred to Southampton in the English Premier League in 2014 as a result of his outstanding achievements. After a while, Sadio transferred to the English Premier League, one of the world's most prominent soccer divisions. In 2016, he signed up with Liverpool FC, a team with a rich history and passionate supporters. As he dazzled the audience with his speed, talent, and goal-scoring prowess, Sadio rapidly established himself as a popular favorite.

But despite his success, Sadio never forgot where he came from. He recalled his early challenges as well as the people who had helped him. He returned to his community by using his newfound fame and money to help others. He helped build a school in his community so that kids there would have the chance to go to school and he has funded hospitals and sports facilities to empower the next generation of dreamers. Additionally, he frequently sends money home to help his family and the residents of Bambali.

Today, Sadio Mané is a household name in football. His journey from the dusty streets of the Senegalese town of Bambali to the grandest stadiums in the world stands as a testament to his unwavering determination, resilience, the power of perseverance, hard work, commitment and the support of his community.

In the end, Sadio's story is not just about soccer. It's about the power of dreams, the value of persistence, and the impact one individual can have when they choose to use their success to uplift others. His journey inspires millions and reminds us that with dedication and the right support, dreams can become reality even when the odds seem insurmountable.

DID YOU KNOW?

Soccer Star Stories:

Lionel Messi: Messi used to get car sick on his way to games as a child, often having to stop the car to avoid vomiting.

Cristiano Ronaldo: Ronaldo's mother used to work as a cook and cleaner at the Sporting Lisbon academy where he trained as a child.

Sadio Mane: Mane made a promise to his father that he wouldn't play professional soccer until he finished his education. He kept that promise and graduated from school before pursuing his soccer career.

Kylian Mbappe: Mbappe's mother, a former professional handball player, helped shape his strong work ethic and discipline from a young age.

Pele: Pele scored his 1,000th goal in a friendly match between Santos and Vasco da Gama. The game was stopped to celebrate his achievement.

Luka Modric: He and his family were refugees during the Croatian War of Independence, living in a hotel as they escaped the conflict.

Andres Iniesta: Iniesta's parents were initially hesitant to let him pursue soccer professionally. They wanted him to focus on his studies, but his talent convinced them otherwise.

Diego Maradona: Maradona's first contract with Barcelona included a clause that allowed him to visit his family in Argentina every three months.

Curious Soccer Facts:

Olympique de L'emyrne, but the goals were all own goals as part of a protest.

The round soccer ball we're familiar with today wasn't used until the 20th century. Earlier balls were more "plum-shaped" and difficult to control.

The World Cup trophy, called the Jules Rimet Trophy, was stolen in 1966 and later found by a dog named "Pickles" in a garden in London.

The game of soccer was banned in England in 1365 by King Edward III because it was deemed too distracting and led to a decline in archery practice.

The longest soccer match ever recorded lasted for 35 hours and 30 minutes.

Soccer balls were originally made using inflated animal bladders, covered in leather.

DAVID BECKHAM

MAIN CAREER HIGHLIGHTS

Premier League: 6

FA Cup: 2

UEFA Champions: 1

Intercont Cup: 1

Spain Super Cup: 1

La Liga: 1

Copa del Rey: 7

MLS Cup: 2

David Beckham: Bend it Like Beckham

On May 2, 1975, a small child by the name of David Robert Joseph Beckham was born amid the busy districts of East London, where the river Thames flows through the metropolis. One of the most recognizable and well-liked soccer stars the world has ever seen was this young child, who had a football at his feet and aspirations in his eyes.

As soon as David could stand, he fell in love with soccer. David's father, a kitchen fitter who loved the game, introduced him to it, and soon the small boy was playing with a ball in the backyard. Every free moment was spent honing his techniques as the ball grew to become an extension of him.

But David's entry into the soccer world was everything but simple. He was raised in a humble environment, and his family couldn't afford expensive soccer equipment. Instead, he practiced his talents with a battered ball while playing in the neighborhood park and on the streets. He was referred as by the neighborhood children as "the boy who could bend the ball like magic."

David's talent grew as he aged and was now too great for the neighborhood park. He joined Manchester United's youth program at the age of 16, one of England's most prominent soccer teams. It was both a struggle and a dream come true. The pressure to succeed at such a young age was enormous, and the competition was strong.

David took on the issues head-on with his renowned work ethic and tenacity. He was aware that skill alone was insufficient; rather, it was his commitment, self-control, and relentless effort that made him stand out. In an effort to become the greatest, he would practice his crosses and free kicks for hours after workouts.

David made his professional debut for Manchester United in 1992 when he was just 17 years old. His transformation into a professional soccer player from a young boy with ambitions was now a reality. But he had only just started his adventure. David's career rose to amazing heights throughout the years. He rose to fame as a result of his accurate passing, exceptional vision, and nearly limitless scoring opportunities. He was a midfielder unlike any other, skilled enough to deftly bend the ball into the net, giving him the moniker "Golden Balls."

But David's status as a world legend was not merely a result of his on-field prowess. Fans all around the world fell in love with him thanks to his style, charisma, and unmistakable appeal. In addition to playing soccer, he was a fashion star, a role model, and a representation of British national pride.

From Manchester United to Real Madrid, the Los Angeles Galaxy in the United States, and even Paris Saint-Germain, David's path carried him. He created a lasting impression at each club, not just for his play on the field but also for his devotion to the group and the supporters.

David kept his roots in mind the entire time he was on his amazing trip. He kept ties to East London, where his family was still residing. He gave back to the community by sponsoring a number of charities and causes using his reputation and wealth. He demonstrated to the entire globe the importance of utilizing prosperity to improve the lives of others in addition to one's own. He has been a UNICEF ambassador to combat child exploitation and health issues in Africa.

Let David Beckham's story motivate you to work tirelessly toward your goals. Let it serve as a reminder that where you're going and the amount of effort, you're prepared to put in to get there matter more than where you came from. David's story is proof that even the most ambitious goals can be achieved with dedication, hard effort, and a never-give-up mentality. Let his path serve as motivation while you pursue your own goals because, like David Beckham, you have the ability to succeed through passion, perseverance, and the conviction that everything is possible.

DID YOU KNOW?

Soccer Star Stories:

Lionel Messi: Messi's favorite dish is Milanese, an Argentine breaded and fried meat dish.

Cristiano Ronaldo: Ronaldo once donated €1.5 million to fund pediatric cancer treatment at a hospital in Portugal.

Sadio Mane: Mane changed his jersey number to 10 for the 2018-2019 season in honor of his childhood idol, Pelé.

Kylian Mbappe: Mbappe once donated all his earnings from the 2018 World Cup to a charity that helps disabled children play sports.

Pele: Pele's name is so iconic that it's been featured in over 1,000 songs worldwide.

Luka Modric: Modric's first job was as a shepherd, where he herded goats in war-torn Croatia.

Sergio Ramos: Ramos has a black belt in karate and is known for his physical style of play.

Diego Maradona: He once worked as a television host on a talk show called "La Noche del 10" (The Night of the 10).

David Beckham: Beckham's most expensive car is a Rolls-Royce Phantom Drophead Coupe.

Mesut Ozil: Ozil is a skilled pianist and often plays the instrument in his free time.

Neymar: Neymar is an avid poker player and has participated in professional poker tournaments.

Curious Soccer Facts:

The oldest soccer club in the world is Sheffield FC, founded in 1857.

The first international soccer match played under floodlights took place in 1878 between England and Scotland.

The highest-scoring soccer match ended with an astonishing 36-0 score. AS Adema defeated Stade

Soccer was included in the Olympics in 1900, but the matches were not recognized as official international matches by FIFA.

The world's first black professional soccer player was Arthur Wharton, who played in the late 1800s.

The heaviest scoreline in a professional soccer match was in 1885 when Arbroath beat Bon Accord 36-0.

LUKA MODRIC

MAIN CAREER HIGHLIGHTS

Croatian Cup: 3

Croatian Super Cup: 1

UEFA Champions: 5

UEFA Super Cup: 4

Spain Super Cup: 4

La Liga: 3

Copa del Rey: 2

Luka Modric: The Midfield Magician's Triumph

In the charming coastal war-torn town of Zadar, Croatia, a young boy named Luka Modric was born on September 9, 1985. As the waves of the Adriatic Sea whispered tales of far-off lands, Luka's own journey was just beginning – a journey that would lead him to conquer soccer's grandest stages and inspire young dreamers everywhere.

Like many young children, Luka's narrative began with a ball at his feet and an endless supply of dreams in his heart. He used the ball as his brush and the streets of Zadar as his canvas to create a work of art that embodied his imagination, zeal, and tenacity. He would pursue the ball from dawn till dusk, honing his passing through confined spaces and daydreaming about playing in front of raucous audiences at stadiums.

But Luka's path to soccer glory was far from a straight line. As a child, he faced adversity that could have deterred his dreams. Croatia was still healing from the wounds of war, and resources were limited. Luka's family lived in a hotel that sheltered refugees during the Croatian War of Independence. The echoes of war were a constant backdrop to his childhood, but amidst the rubble and ruins, Luka found his playground. He would kick around a makeshift ball, his tiny feet creating a rhythm that drowned out the sounds of war. His passion for soccer was evident even then. Despite the hardships, he always had a smile on his face, a soccer ball at his feet, and dreams in his heart. Soccer shoes were a luxury, and the fields he played on were often more rugged than refined. Yet, in the face of these challenges, Luka's spirit remained unbroken, his feet dancing with the rhythm of his dreams.

It was evident that Luka had potential. He started playing soccer at the young age of six with NK Zadar, a local team. His abilities and tenacity amazed his coaches. Luka was unstoppable despite his little stature and the impending conflict. Long after his colleagues had left for the night, he would frequently be spotted working out in the moonlight. But Luka's path wasn't without difficulties. His family was struggling to make ends meet, let alone pay for soccer equipment. Luka, though, was certain. If need be, he would play barefoot, which he frequently did.

His persistence paid off when, at the age of 16, scouts saw Luka's skill and accepted him into Dinamo Zagreb's junior program. It was a dream come true, but it was also a reminder of the fierce competition he faced. He was no longer the largest fish in a little pond, but rather a small fish circling around other up-and-coming artists who were equally driven to succeed. Luka practiced more diligently than ever, sometimes being the last person on the field. He finally attracted the interest of foreign teams because to his hard work, talent, and devotion, which drove him to the pinnacle of Croatian soccer.

Luka's reserved nature made his journey even more daunting. He wasn't the tallest or the loudest on the field, but what he lacked in physical presence, he more than compensated for with his intelligence and determination. He understood the game on a level that set him apart, reading plays, anticipating movements, and orchestrating the flow of the game like a maestro.

As Luka's abilities increased, he encountered another obstacle. His progress was in danger of being stopped by an injury, which raised concerns about his future. However, Luka's journey was characterized by tenacity. He committed himself to recovery, leveraging the setback to become more resilient and driven than ever.

Luka rose through the ranks because to his talent and perseverance, making his Croatian national team debut in 2008 as a result. Being able to represent his nation on a world scale gave him a great sense of pride. But Luka understood that the adventure was only beginning a new stage and was far from done.

When he joined Tottenham Hotspur in the English Premier League in 2008, his career underwent a significant shift. The world was about to see Luka Modric's genius on a large stage. His on-field performances were a symphony of talent, exact passes, and exceptional vision. He developed into a midfield wizard, able to change the course of a game with only one touch of the ball. He amazed the people with his abilities and rapidly won over the crowd. And as he soared to new heights, he never forgot his roots. He remained connected to his homeland, using his influence to inspire young soccer players in Croatia. He regularly contributes to charities in Croatia and helps young athletes in his hometown.

The pinnacle of Luka's journey came in the 2018 FIFA World Cup. He led Croatia to the final, a feat that captured the world's attention and ignited a sense of national pride. Though they fell short of victory, Luka's impact went beyond the scoresheet. He had shown that a small country with a big heart could compete at the highest level, proving that dreams could be realized through determination and teamwork. He even won the Golden Ball as the tournament's best player becoming the first player other than Lionel Messi or Cristiano Ronaldo to win it in a decade.

Luka's story was one of triumph over challenges, of a quiet determination that spoke volumes on the field. As you follow his journey, let it remind you that size and circumstance are not barriers to success. Let Luka's journey inspire you to chase your aspirations with relentless determination, to overcome setbacks with resilience, and to use your talents to make a positive impact in the world. Like Luka, you have the power to achieve greatness through dedication, hard work, and the unwavering belief that with perseverance, even the loftiest dreams can come true.

DID YOU KNOW?

Soccer Star Stories:

Lionel Messi: Messi once auctioned his famous left foot cast, which he used after a fracture, and the funds raised were donated to a children's hospital.

Cristiano Ronaldo: Ronaldo is known for his rigorous workout routines; he reportedly does 3,000 sit-ups every day.

Sadio Mane: Mane's father initially opposed his soccer aspirations and wanted him to become a scholar. They later reconciled when his talent became evident.

Kylian Mbappe: Mbappe's father, a soccer coach, often disguised himself with a hood and sunglasses to watch Kylian play without drawing attention.

Pele: Pele scored his 1,000th goal on November 19, 1969, with a historic free-kick, making him the only player to reach that milestone.

Luka Modric: Modric's mother worked as a textile worker and later opened a fruit stand to support her family during the war in Croatia.

Andres Iniesta: Iniesta's father was a well-known businessman in their small village, and the community raised funds to help him afford his first pair of soccer boots.

Diego Maradona: Maradona's mother had a strong influence on his love for soccer, even sewing soccer balls for him when he was a child.

Curious Soccer Facts:

The world's oldest soccer competition is the FA Cup, first contested in 1871-1872.

In 1950, the United States defeated England in the World Cup with a makeshift team, as most of their best players declined the invitation.

Soccer was played in the Olympics as early as 1900, but it wasn't until 1908 that it was included as an official sport.

In 1995, Cameroon's Marc-Vivien Foé scored a goal and then proceeded to propose to his girlfriend during a match.

The term "soccer" originated from the sport's full name, "association football," where players would be called "assoc" for short and then "soccer."

The fastest goal in Premier League history was scored by Shane Long of Southampton in just 7.69 seconds against Watford in 2019.

KYLIAN MBAPPE

MAIN CAREER HIGHLIGHTS

World Cup: 1

UEFA Nations Ligue: 1

UEFA Europe U19: 1

Ligue 1 (France): 5

Coupe de France: 3

Coupe Ligue: 2

Tropee Champ: 2

Kylian Mbappé: The Unstoppable Rise of a Soccer Prodigy

In the heart of France, just outside Paris, in the charming town of Bondy, a young boy named Kylian Mbappé was born on December 20, 1998. Little did the world know that this unassuming boy would grow up to become a soccer sensation, capturing hearts with his dazzling skills and inspiring countless dreamers to pursue their aspirations against all odds. Kylian was not an ordinary child; he was gifted with extraordinary speed and agility.

Kylian's parents, who are both athletes, spotted their son's potential and signed him up for the neighborhood soccer team, AS Bondy. Here, Kylian's abilities were sharpened in front of his coach and father, Wilfried, who kept a close eye on him. Kylian was the team's youngest member, but his ability was obvious. He had a propensity for scoring goals and was quick and nimble.

But life wasn't all smooth passes and perfect strikes for Kylian. He was often overlooked due to his young age and small stature. Many doubted his ability to compete against older, stronger players. But Kylian was not deterred. He used these criticisms as fuel to work harder, train longer, and prove his doubters wrong. Also, Bondy, though rich in passion, was limited in resources. Shoes were worn, fields were uneven, and opportunities were far from abundant. Yet, these challenges only fueled Kylian's determination to rise above the odds and show the world what he was made of.

Former professional soccer player Wilfried Mbappé, his father, could see the passion in his son's eyes. He became Kylian's mentor, encouraging his potential and assisting in his skill-building. Together, they developed a training program that put Kylian to the limit by having him dribble through small areas, practice precision passes, and perfecting his striking ability. Their common love of the game served as a motivating factor in shaping Kylian's future.

With age, Kylian made noticeable progress on the soccer pitch. He joined neighborhood teams, leaving his imprint after each game. His reading of the game was remarkable, and his pace was astounding. But there were obstacles along the way to the top. Kylian had setbacks and disappointments, but his attitude was unwavering. He was prepared to put in the effort necessary to demonstrate his value since he was aware that the road to success was paved with tenacity.

A scout from the elite Claire Fontaine academy once noticed Kylian playing in a nearby game. The scout gave Kylian a position in the academy after being impressed by his abilities. Even though it was his dream come true, Kylian had to say goodbye to his loved ones. Despite the challenges, Kylian seized the chance because he knew it was a step in realizing his ambition.

Kylian's talent grew throughout his time at Claire Fontaine. He competed against the greatest young players in France and trained with some of the best coaches in the nation. His dedication paid off, as at the age of just 16, he was recruited by the senior squad of AS Monaco, one of the greatest professional soccer clubs in France. The shift to professional soccer was like entering a new planet where there was plenty of fierce and tough competition. Kylian's debut was the start of a stratospheric climb that astounded onlookers. His abilities to go past opponents and his precise finishing were more akin to those of an experienced veteran than a young player.

Kylian's rise to stardom was meteoric. He helped Monaco win the French league title and reach the semi-finals of the Champions League. His performances caught the attention of Paris Saint-Germain (PSG), one of the world's biggest soccer clubs. PSG signed Kylian for a record-breaking fee, making him the most expensive teenage player in history.

In the summer of 2018, Kylian's path took an extraordinary turn. He represented France at the FIFA World Cup, an event when sportsmen and nations' aspirations came together. Kylian delivered performances that were nothing short of remarkable when the entire world was watching him. His lightning-quick movement left opponents in the dust, and his goals sparked international jubilation.

But amidst the spotlight and celebrations, Kylian remained grounded. He understood the significance of his roots and the people who had believed in him from the beginning. He returned to Bondy not as a soccer superstar, but as a hometown hero who had achieved the extraordinary. He knew that his journey was a source of inspiration for the children who shared his dream, and he was determined to use his platform to make a difference.

Giving back to others became a cornerstone of Kylian's quest. He utilized his clout to promote programs that emphasized the health and education of children. According to him, success was more than simply one's own accomplishments; it also involved having a beneficial influence on other people. His deeds revealed much about his personality and his faith in the virtue of compassion.

So, dear readers, as you follow Kylian Mbappé's journey, remember that dreams are worth chasing, regardless of the obstacles you encounter. Let his story inspire you to work diligently toward your aspirations, overcome challenges with resilience, and never forget the importance of giving back to your community. Like Kylian, you have the potential to make your dreams a reality, leaving an indelible mark on the world through your passion, dedication, and the kindness you share.

DID YOU KNOW?

Soccer Star Stories:

Lionel Messi: Messi's first agent, who helped him secure a contract with FC Barcelona, was also his father's close friend.

Cristiano Ronaldo: Ronaldo is an accomplished swimmer and was awarded the title of "Madeira's Best Swimmer of All Time" in 2014.

Sadio Mane: Growing up, Mane's family couldn't afford a television, so he would watch soccer games through the windows of electronic stores.

Kylian Mbappe: Mbappe donated his entire World Cup salary to a charity organization that helps children with disabilities play sports.

Pele: Pele is an honorary citizen of more than 60 cities around the world due to his impact on the sport.

Luka Modric: Modric's idol growing up was Zvonimir Boban, a Croatian soccer legend who later became his national team coach.

Andres Iniesta: Iniesta's wife is his childhood sweetheart whom he met at the age of 12.

Diego Maradona: Maradona's jersey number, 10, was chosen for him by his coach when he joined Argentinos Juniors because the number 10 shirt was the only one available.

Curious Soccer Facts:

The fastest goal ever scored in an official soccer match was in 2004 by Nawaf Al Abed of Al Hilal in just 2 seconds.

The largest soccer stadium in the world is Rungrado 1st of May Stadium in North Korea, with a seating capacity of 114,000.

The fastest red card in a World Cup match was given to Jose Batista of Uruguay in 1986 after just 56 seconds for a foul against Scotland.

In 1998, a French soccer team named FC Vendenheim played against another French team, AS Illzach Modenheim, with a record-breaking 13 players.

The fastest hattrick in soccer history was scored by Tommy Ross in just 90 seconds during a Scottish league match in 1964.

The first soccer match played in space was between astronauts Aleksandr Skvortsov and Oleg Artemyev on the International Space Station in 2014.

DIEGO A. MARADONA

MAIN CAREER HIGHLIGHTS

World Cup: 1

UEFA Cup: 1

Serie A: 2

Coppa Italiana: 1

Super Coppa Ital: 1

La Liga: 1

Copa del Rey: 1

Artemio Franchi: 1

Diego Maradona: The Legend Who Soared

On October 30, 1960, a small kid named Diego Armando Maradona entered the world in the busy neighborhoods of Lanus, Argentina. Diego's upbringing in a low-income household made life difficult for him. In the Villa Fiorito slum, where dreams often remained just that - dreams. Little did anybody realize that this young child would grow up in Argentina's bustling streets and passionate soccer culture to become one of the sport's most famous players ever, a legend whose path would inspire future generations.

But Diego was different. He had a dream, and he was determined to make it a reality. His dream was to play soccer, not just in the dusty lanes of his neighborhood, but on the lush green fields of the world's best stadiums.

Diego first developed a passion for soccer when he was just three years old. His cousin had given him his first soccer ball, which he would spend hours kicking about as his little feet made lovely melody with the ball. His skill was obvious by the time he was eight. During a street game, a scout from one of the neighborhood clubs, Argentinos Juniors, came across him and was pleased by his abilities. His entry into the professional soccer league began when he accepted an invitation to play for the club's junior squad.

But Diego's journey was not without its obstacles. Raised in a humble family, he faced challenges that could have stifled his dreams. Diego had to juggle school, soccer practice, and helping his family make ends meet. But he never complained. He believed that every drop of sweat, every bruise, every struggle was a stepping stone towards his dream. The odds were stacked against him, yet his determination burned brighter than ever. He knew that soccer was his ticket to a better life, his means of rising above the circumstances that surrounded him. And so, with a heart full of hope and a spirit that refused to be defeated, Diego pressed forward.

As he honed his skills, Diego faced doubts about his stature. His diminutive frame led skeptics to question whether he could compete on the global stage dominated by taller players. But Diego was no ordinary player – he possessed a magic that went beyond height or physicality. His agility, speed, and unmatched creativity set him apart, making him a force to be reckoned with.

His hard work paid off when, at just 15 years old, Diego made his professional debut for Argentinos Juniors. He was the youngest player in the history of Argentine Primera Division. His skill on the field was mesmerizing, and he quickly became a sensation. The world was about to witness the birth of a phenomenon. His skill on the field was mesmerizing, as he effortlessly maneuvered past defenders, leaving them in awe of his grace and finesse. The streets of Argentina buzzed with excitement, and the legend of Maradona began to take shape.

Diego's adventure culminated in a thrilling FIFA World Cup that was staged in Mexico in 1986. He put on performances as the representative of Argentina that cemented his place in soccer history. He achieved what is sometimes referred to as the "Goal of the Century" during this competition, a brilliant solo run that displayed his extraordinary skill and left the world in awe. He is still remembered for his notorious "Hand of God" goal and his incredible solo goal against England in the quarterfinals. He was a hero, a legend, and a genuine sports superstar. Argentina won because to his foresight, originality, and brave play, and he was hailed as a national hero.

Diego's tale, however, was not without its complications. He suffered from the strain of fame and the burden of expectations. His struggles and obstacles in life threatened to eclipse his accomplishments. But despite the difficulties, his willpower never wavered. He demonstrated to the world that strength could come from weakness and that the road to greatness was frequently lined with both victories and hardships.

Diego maintained a connection to his roots despite receiving widespread praise. He recognized the importance of his origins and the influence his upbringing had on him. He invested in neighborhood initiatives and supported charities that assisted the impoverished and the destitute while also using his influence to promote social justice. His voyage served as a reminder that success meant more than simply achieving one's own goals; it also meant affecting good change for others around you.

Beyond his playing career, Diego left a lasting legacy. He changed careers and started coaching, passing along his expertise and love of the sport to younger players. He never stopped inspiring both players and spectators, serving as a live example of how goals can come true with perseverance, hard effort, and an unwavering passion for the game.

But Diego's story was not without its complexities. The pressures of fame and the weight of expectations took a toll on him. He faced personal battles and challenges that threatened to overshadow his achievements. Yet, even in moments of adversity, his determination remained unbroken. He showed the world that strength could emerge from vulnerability, and that the journey to greatness was often paved with both triumphs and tribulations.

Despite the global acclaim, Diego remained connected to his roots. He understood the significance of where he came from and the role his upbringing played in shaping him. He used his influence to advocate for social justice and to give back to his community, investing in local projects and supporting charities that helped the poor and the underprivileged. His journey was a reminder that success was not just about personal achievement, but about creating positive change for others.

Diego's legacy extended beyond his playing days. He transitioned into coaching, sharing his knowledge and passion for the game with the next generation. He continued to inspire players and fans alike, a living testament to the idea that dreams could be realized through hard work, resilience, and a never-ending love for the game.

At the pinnacle of his success, Diego once said, "I am Maradona, who makes goals, who makes mistakes. I can take it all, I have shoulders big enough to fight with everybody." He was a fighter, on and off the field, never shying away from standing up for what he believed in.

Diego Maradona's story is a testament to the power of dreams, hard work, and perseverance. His journey from the shantytowns of Buenos Aires to the world's biggest soccer stadiums is an inspiration for every child who dares to dream.

As you dive into Diego Maradona's story, let it serve as a reminder that no dream is too big to chase. Let his journey inspire you to pursue your aspirations with unwavering determination, to overcome challenges with courage, and to use your talents to make a positive impact in the world. Like Diego, you have the power to rise above circumstances, to embrace your uniqueness, and to achieve greatness through perseverance and a never-ending passion for what you love.

DID YOU KNOW?

Soccer Star Stories:

Lionel Messi: Messi's first contract with FC Barcelona was written on a napkin by his father and Barcelona's sporting director, Carles Rexach, during a restaurant meeting.

Cristiano Ronaldo: Ronaldo once paid for the medical bills of a young fan's brain surgery, after learning about his condition.

Sadio Mane: Mane donated $200,000 to build a school and mosque in his hometown in Senegal, focusing on education for children.

Kylian Mbappe: Mbappe became the youngest French player to score in a World Cup at the age of 19 during the 2018 tournament.

Pele: Pele is known to have scored over 1,000 official goals in his career, but the exact number is disputed due to different criteria for counting goals.

Luka Modric: Modric's rise to fame was depicted in a Croatian documentary called "Luka," highlighting his journey from war-torn streets to soccer stardom.

Andres Iniesta: Iniesta owns a winery named Bodega Iniesta, producing a variety of wines.

Diego Maradona: Maradona is also remembered for his passion for chess and even played against former world chess champion Anatoly Karpov.

Curious Soccer Facts:

The longest penalty shootout in professional soccer history occurred in 2005, when the Namibian Cup final was decided by 48 penalty kicks.

In 1970, El Salvador forfeited a World Cup match against Haiti, leading to the highest-scoring World Cup match ever, with Haiti winning 4-0.

During the 1950 World Cup, the United States defeated England 1-0 in a match known as the "Miracle on Grass."

The only soccer player to win three World Cups is Pelé, who achieved this feat in 1958, 1962, and 1970 with Brazil.

The largest soccer tournament in the world is the Gothia Cup in Sweden, with over 1,600 teams from more than 80 countries participating.

A British prisoner of war in World War II escaped from a camp by playing soccer with the guards and then simply walking away.

NEYMAR DA SILVA JR.

MAIN CAREER HIGHLIGHTS

Summer Olympics: 1	Copa del Rey: 3
FIFA Confed Cup: 1	Ligue 1 (France): 5
UEFA Champions: 1	Coupe de France: 3
Spain Super Cup: 1	Coupe Ligue: 2
La Liga: 2	Trophee Champ: 3

Neymar Jr.: The Samba Superstar's Journey

In the vibrant streets of Mogi das Cruzes, Brazil, a young boy named Neymar da Silva Santos Junior, with a mop of curly hair and boundless energy, was born on February 5, 1992. Little did anyone know that this spirited boy, who grew up playing soccer barefoot in the favelas, would become one of the most electrifying soccer stars the world had ever seen.

Neymar's story began in a humble neighborhood, where soccer wasn't just a sport; it was a way of life. The dusty streets and improvised goals were his playground, and the joy of the game was the soundtrack of his childhood. From the moment he could walk, he had a ball at his feet, and his dreams soared higher than the rooftops of the favela.

But Neymar's journey into the world of soccer was far from a smooth ride. His family didn't have much, and buying soccer shoes or jerseys was a luxury they couldn't afford. Yet, his passion for the game burned brighter than any hardship. He would tie his shoelaces together to keep the shoes from falling apart, all the while honing his dazzling skills.

Neymar's brilliance grew too great for the favela as he got older. He left home at the age of 11 to join the youth program of legendary Brazilian soccer team Santos FC. Although it was a difficult choice that required Neymar to say goodbye to his family and friends, he understood it was the first step in achieving his goals.

Neymar experienced a lot of opposition in the youth academy. His very fragile body cast doubt on his capacity to succeed in the world of professional soccer. He possessed a special left foot, lightning-quick dribbling, and a penchant for the unexpected, but he also had something more that made him stand out. He put out great effort to demonstrate his conviction that brilliance could transcend any challenge.

Neymar made his professional debut for Santos FC in 2009, kicking off his ascent to fame. His performances were exceptional in every way. He scored stunning goals, effortlessly dribbled past defenders, and won over the spectators with his brand of play. He was the newest soccer phenomenon in Brazil.

Neymar was under a lot of strain and public criticism as his fame grew. The pressure of what the public and the media expected of him acted as a second defense attempting to stop him. However, Neymar accepted the pressure with his recognizable smile and unwavering confidence. He was aware that every obstacle presented a chance for improvement.

Neymar moved to Barcelona, one of the most prominent clubs in Europe, in 2013, causing quite a stir. Although he played with soccer greats like Lionel Messi and Andres Iniesta, he didn't cower in their presence. Rather, he flourished. He formed one of the most fearsome attacking trios in the world alongside Messi and Suarez.

Neymar realized a longtime goal in 2016 as he assisted Brazil in winning the Olympic gold at the Rio Games. Neymar's tears of delight demonstrated how much the event meant to him and how much it meant to his country. He dedicated the win to his people in honor of keeping his commitment to them.

Neymar's journey was characterized by humility as much as achievement. He never lost sight of his roots despite achieving fame and wealth. He still had a strong bond with his family and the slum where he was raised. He made a difference in his community by supporting charitable endeavors and soccer camps for needy kids. He contributed enormously for the Ebola's campaign, also had helped to bring potable water to very poor regions in Brazil.

Don't forget about the youngster from the favela who dared to dream while you read about Neymar's journey. Let his example motivate you to pursue your goals with unyielding tenacity. Let it serve as a reminder to you that no challenge is insurmountable and that ability and perseverance make a potent combination.

You have the ability, like Neymar, to overcome obstacles, follow your aspirations, and utilize your success to change the world for the better. Neymar's path is evidence that even the most ambitious goals can be achieved with dedication, hard effort, and a never-give-up mindset.

CONCLUSION

In the world of soccer, where dreams are scored and legends are made, we've embarked on an incredible journey through the lives of eleven remarkable stars. We've seen them soar to astonishing heights, but what truly sets them apart is not just their skill on the field, but their hearts off it.

These soccer heroes, from humble beginnings, faced hardships that would've felled lesser spirits. They knew the sting of defeat and the bitter taste of setbacks. But they never gave up. They kicked down doors that blocked their path to glory. They rose, again and again, with unwavering determination.

Yet, their stories are not just about personal triumphs. They are about the unbreakable bonds they share with their roots, the communities that nurtured their dreams. These stars never forgot where they came from, the people who believed in them when the world doubted. They remind us that true success isn't just about glory and riches; it's about giving back, about remembering the hearts that beat alongside us.

Dear young readers, these stories are more than just tales of soccer triumphs; they are blueprints for your own dreams. These soccer stars were once kids like you, with big dreams and small beginnings. They didn't let their shortcomings and struggles define them. Instead, they used them as stepping stones, as fuel for their determination.

As you turn the final page of this book, remember this: life won't always be easy, but it's your response to challenges that will shape your destiny. The lesson from these stars is clear—hard work, persistence, and the unwavering belief in your dreams can turn them into reality.

So, take their stories to heart. Let them inspire you. When you face your own obstacles, think of how these legends overcame theirs. Keep this book as your guide, a constant reminder that greatness can be achieved through dedication and resilience.

As you chase your dreams, remember the communities that support you, the people who believe in you. Just like these soccer stars, let your success shine a light on those around you. Be the hero of your own story, and when you reach your goals, never forget to reach back and help others along the way.

Now, I invite you to take the next step on your journey, to be inspired by the lives of these soccer stars, to learn from their struggles and their triumphs. Purchase this book, not just as a story to read, but as a landmark of your own progress towards your dreams. Let it be a constant source of motivation and a reminder that with hard work and a heart full of determination, you can achieve greatness and make your own mark on the world.

The world is waiting for the next generation of stars. Will you be one of them? The choice is yours. Go, chase your dreams, and never forget where you came from.

Disclaimer

This book is written with young readers in mind and it hopes to motivate and inspire them to pursue their dreams and aspirations, work hard in life and overcome struggles. Any decisions or actions taken in reliance on the information contained in this book are not the author's responsibility.

Thank you for choosing us, we value your Amazon review immensely. Your thoughts and feedback are highly appreciated. Thank you for taking the time to share!

Made in United States
North Haven, CT
28 November 2023

44710249R00054